Vol. 1

Swear And Relax

Swear Word
Adult Coloring Book

Download free coloring pages at
www.swearandrelax.com

piss off

Assmunch

Kiss my
shiny ass

I don't give a damn

Bellend

clusterfuck

Damnit

What the fuck
did I just read?

Bastard

Calm the
fuck down!

Cozy

Bullshit

I am sick
of this
Shit

Bloody Hell

tt

Bitch

Dumbass

Asshat

Muckspout

Bunghole

FUCK

WHAT THE HELL?

Prick

Shut the fuck up!

Shit happens

50713936R00031

Made in the USA
Lexington, KY
27 March 2016